Grow Your Own
Cat Toy

John Malam

Heinemann Library
Chicago, Illinois

www.heinemannraintree.com
Visit our website to find out more information about Heinemann-Raintree books.

To order:
☎ Phone 888-454-2279
▭ Visit www.heinemannraintree.com to browse our catalog and order online.

© 2012 Heinemann Library
an imprint of Capstone Global Library, LLC
Chicago, Illinois

Edited by Daniel Nunn, Rebecca Rissman, and Sian Smith
Designed by Philippa Jenkins
Picture research by Mica Brancic
Originated by Capstone Global Library Ltd
Printed and bound in China by Leo Paper Products Ltd

15 14 13 12 11
10 9 8 7 6 5 4 3 2 1

Library of Congress Cataloging-in-Publication Data
Malam, John, 1957-
  Grow your own cat toy / John Malam.
      p. cm.—(Grow it yourself!)
  Includes bibliographical references and index.
  ISBN 978-1-4329-5110-8 (hc)—ISBN 978-1-4329-5117-7
(pb) 1. Catnip—Juvenile literature. 2. Toys for cats—Juvenile literature. I. Title.
  QK495.L25M35 2012
  636.8—dc22   2010049835

Acknowledgments
The author and publisher are grateful to the following for permission to reproduce copyright material: Alamy pp. 5 (© amandacat), 7 (© Antje Schulte - Insects), 10 (© Andreas Keuchel), 11 (© Juniors Bildarchiv), 18 (© Andrea Jones), 23 (© David Askham); Ardea pp. 9 (© Ardea London), 15 (© David Dixon); © Capstone Global Library Ltd p. 13 bottom (Philippa Jenkins); © Capstone Publishers pp. 28, 29 (Karon Dubke); GAP Photos p. 21 (Graham Strong); Garden World Images pp. 24, 25, 26, 27 (N. Colborn); Getty Images pp. 8 (GAP Photos/Clive Nichols), 14 (UpperCut Images/Robert Houser), 17 (Image Source); Photolibrary p. 12 (Garden Picture Library/Ron Evans); Science Photo Library p. 4 (J B Rapkins); Shutterstock pp. 6 (© Richard Oechsner), 13 top (© Bonchan), 16 (© pixmac), 19 (© Elnur), 20 (© Naaman Abreu), 22 (© Thomas Oswald).

Cover photographs of Nepeta nervosa 'Pink cat' (Catmint, catnip) reproduced with permission of Photolibrary (Garden Picture Library/Howard Rice), and a hand-made cat toy reproduced with permission of © Capstone Publishers (Karon Dubke).

To find out about the author, visit his website:
www.johnmalam.co.uk

Every effort has been made to contact copyright holders of any material reproduced in this book. Any omissions will be rectified in subsequent printings if notice is given to the publisher.

All the Internet addresses (URLs) given in this book were valid at the time of going to press. However, due to the dynamic nature of the Internet, some addresses may have changed, or sites may have changed or ceased to exist since publication. While the author and publisher regret any inconvenience this may cause readers, no responsibility for any such changes can be accepted by either the author or the publisher.

Some words are shown in bold, **like this**. You can find out what they mean by looking in the glossary.

Contents

Note to adults:

There are many varieties of catnip. Cats are particularly attracted to *Nepeta cataria*, and this is the plant you should use. *Nepeta x faassenii* is an ornamental plant and is less attractive to cats.

What Is Catnip?

Catnip is a plant. It is also called catmint. Catnip is very useful. Its leaves can be used to make tea. Catnip can also be used to help people with colds and upset stomachs to feel better.

There are many types of catnip, but the type cats like best is called *Nepeta cataria.*

This cat is rolling on young catnip plants.

Cats love catnip! They like its smell. They rub against the plant and bite its leaves. Dried catnip is put into toys for cats to play with. It is not only pet cats that like catnip. Lions, tigers, and other big cats like it, too.

Catnip Close Up

Catnip is a bushy plant with gray-green leaves. The leaves are oval, have **serrated** edges, and end in a point. The **stems** and leaves are covered in little hairs.

serrated edges

stem

This bee is drinking nectar from a catnip flower.

Catnip plants grow to about 24 inches high. They make flowers in the summer. The flowers can be white or purple. Bees love to crawl into the flowers to feed on the **nectar**.

Why Do Cats Like Catnip?

Catnip plants make a special type of **oil**. When cats smell the oil, it makes them think of other cats. They become very playful.

Cats love the smell of catnip.

This cat has found some catnip plants!

Cats bite catnip leaves and roll around in the plants. They do this to crush the plants. It makes the plants **release** more of their oil. Cats go crazy for catnip!

Catnip and Your Cat

Catnip can be used as a treat for a cat. Pet stores sell sprays that smell like catnip. It can be sprayed onto a cat's **scratching post**. The cat will love to scratch and nibble at the post.

scratching post

A little pillow filled with dried catnip makes a great toy for a cat to play with.

Catnip leaves can be dried and put into toys for cats. Cats love to play with catnip toys. They nibble at them and carry them around the house. You can make a catnip toy for a cat you know.

Grow Your Own Catnip

It is easy to grow catnip. The plants will grow almost anywhere. They need very little care, and very little water.

This catnip is growing in a flower bed.

catnip

baby catnip plant

catnip seeds

CATMINT

ENJOYED BY CATS EVERYWHERE!

You can buy packs of catnip **seeds** and baby catnip plants at a plant nursery. Once you have catnip growing in your yard, it will come up again year after year.

Where to Grow Catnip

Catnip grows outside. You can grow it in a **flower bed**, or in a large plant pot. It likes to grow in a sunny place. It does not like to be in the **shade**.

It does not take long for baby catnip plants to grow.

If you don't want catnip to spread as much as this, you can grow it in a pot instead.

Catnip spreads. Each year it makes new plants, which cover more and more ground. Choose a growing area you don't mind it spreading over.

Grow Catnip from Seed

In early spring, clear the growing area of weeds. Then, make a **seed bed** to **sow** your catnip **seeds** in. Loosen the soil with a gardening fork. Break up any lumps. Rake over the area to remove rocks.

Pull a rake across the soil to catch rocks and move them out of the way.

seed bed

Sow catnip seeds by scattering them across the surface of the soil.

Pour a few seeds into your hand. Take little pinches of the seeds and **scatter** them across the seed bed. Use a rake to mix the seeds into the soil. Sprinkle water over the soil with a watering can.

Watering the Seed Bed

Keep the **seed bed** watered, specially in dry weather. Try not to let the soil dry out or the **seeds** will not grow. If it has been raining, the rain will have done the watering for you.

Use a sprinkler head to sprinkle water gently over the seed bed.

sprinkler head

Seedlings have tiny leaves and **stems**.

After two or three weeks, look out for the tiny leaves of the first **seedlings**. It is often easier to spot them after the soil has been watered.

Too Many Plants!

If all the **seeds** grow, you will have too many plants. The growing area will become overcrowded. The plants won't like it. You need to **thin** them out when they are little.

These catnip plants are growing too close to each other.

Catnip plants need room to grow.

When the plants are about 4 inches high, decide which ones to keep. They should be about 12 inches apart. Pull up the ones you don't want and put them into your **compost pile**.

Stay Away Cats!

Cats will soon find out that you are growing catnip. They will sneak into your yard, nibble the plants, and roll around in them. This is fun to watch.

Cats can often smell catnip from far away.

Garden netting will keep the cats away!

Cats can make a mess of your plants. If you cover the plants with garden **netting**, cats will stay away from the plants.

23

Harvesting Your Catnip

By the middle of summer, catnip is fully grown. It is time to **harvest** the leaves. Ask an adult to cut the **stems** about 8 inches from the ground. You will need lots of leaves, so cut lots of stems.

Ask an adult to cut the catnip for you.

Pull the leaves off the stems and put them on a tray. Put the tray on a windowsill and leave it for a few days so that the leaves can dry out.

Crush the Leaves

When the leaves are completely dry, they will be **brittle**. Put them into a big bowl. Crunch them up and rub them together with your hands.

Dried catnip leaves look like this.

Rub the leaves with your hands. This breaks them into tiny pieces. ▼

Breaking the leaves into tiny pieces helps to **release** the smell of the catnip.

Make a Catnip Toy

Now you can use your catnip to make a ball for a cat to play with. Please ask an adult to help you with this activity.

You will need:
an old sock
scissors
a needle
thread
dried catnip leaves
a piece of string about 3 feet long.

1. Cut the toe end off the sock.
   It should be about 4 inches long.
2. Fill the toe with the crushed catnip
   leaves until it starts to become
   round, like a ball.
3. Ask an adult to sew the open end
   of the sock to close it.
4. Tie the string onto the sock. Your
   cat toy is finished!

Glossary

brittle something that breaks or snaps easily

compost pile heap of old plants, grass cuttings, and leaves which are left to rot down

flower bed part of a yard where flowers grow

harvest to gather fruit and vegetables when they are ready to pick or dig up

nectar sugary liquid made by plants

netting plastic net with holes in it

oil type of liquid

release to let go of something

scatter to spread seeds across an area by throwing them

scratching post post for a cat to scratch on

seed part of a plant that grows into a new plant

seed bed area of fine soil where seeds are sown

seedling baby plant

serrated having a notched or jagged edge

shade darker area of the yard, where trees or buildings cast shadows

sow to plant a seed

stem main branch or trunk of a plant

thin to remove unwanted plants so that the rest of the plants have more space

Find Out More

Books to read

Grow It, Eat It. New York: Dorling Kindersley, 2008.

Websites

www.bluebirdgardens.com/?realm=Cats&page=Catnip
Find out lots of information about catnip and how to make catnip toys on this Website.

www.kiddiegardens.com
This Website will give you lots of ideas on how to grow plants that you can use to make things.

www.thekidsgarden.co.uk
Discover more gardening ideas and activities on this Website.

Index